Formatting Manuscripts
for Submission to
Publishers and Agents
Microsoft Word 2010 (2007)

Formatting Manuscripts

for Submission to

Publishers and Agents
Microsoft Word 2010 (2007)

By
Kate Jonez

OG Writer's Guides
Los Angeles CA

Formatting Manuscripts for Submission to Publishers and Agents
Microsoft Word 2010 (2007)
Copyright © 2013 Kate Jonez

ISBN-13: 978-0615767024
ISBN-10: 0615767028

All rights reserved. No part of this book may be reproduced or transmitted in any form or by any electronic or mechanical means, including photocopying, recording or by any information storage and retrieval system, without the written permission of the author and publisher.

First Edition

Introduction

This book is a concise easy-to-read guide that explains step by step how to correctly format a document according to publisher's guidelines. For the purposes of this book, I am using guidelines that are common with many publishers.

Once a novel or short story is complete and is finally ready to submit to a publisher or agent, a writer can take one final step to ensure the manuscript gets the attention it deserves. A beautifully formatted manuscript has an advantage. Of course, the story and the quality of the writing is what will ultimately lead to a sale, but in a competitive market, writers who give their manuscript extra care and attention have a better chance of getting publishers to read their work.

Formatting counts. A writer who takes the time to present a correctly formatted document that follows the publisher's guidelines stands out as a professional. Do publishers notice? I can say from experience, yes. As chief editor at Omnium Gatherum, I look at manuscripts all day long. Whether I'm editing, formatting for print or ebook or proofreading galleys, all of the documents I work with have a uniform look. My eyes are used to this. When I receive a submission that fits with my work flow, I concentrate on the writing. When I receive a wonky one, I'm annoyed and I also think about how much extra time I'm going to have to spend to teach this writer (who obviously is not very good at following instructions) how to use writing software.

Most publishers list formatting requirements in their guidelines. When approaching a market, follow these guidelines— exactly. One size does not fit all. If a publisher requests a particular font, use it. If they request three-quarter inch margins, don't submit a document with one inch margins because that's what you have. Format the document for each publisher individually or your manuscript will stand out as the one that doesn't fit.

Most formatting guidelines for US publishers (Slight variations for other countries) look something like this:

Standard Manuscript Guidelines

- Letter-size **pages** 81/2 x 11
- 1 inch **margins**
- 12 point serif **font** (Times Roman or Courier)
- **Double-spaced**
- First word of a paragraph **indented** .5 (1/2) inch
- **No spaces** between paragraphs
- Numbered **pages**
- **Author information** including name, address, phone number, and email address in the top left corner of the first page (single-spaced)
- Author name and book title in the **header** and the title of manuscript on the first page

Many of these guidelines are vestiges of a time when manuscripts were submitted on paper. (Perhaps they don't even make much sense for documents read primarily on a computer screen).The reason for any particular requirement, however, should not be the writer's concern. The goal of the guidelines is to have all submissions formatted the same. The most important objective is to follow the guidelines exactly.

In addition to a following a publisher's guidelines, writers should also demonstrate that they know how to use word processing software. Microsoft Word is the standard. (Although OpenOffice/LibreOffice also produces acceptable documents) Word has a large number of features that are beyond the scope of this book. Many are designed for business use and are of little use to a creative writer when formatting a manuscript. Others are very helpful. When writers use the features of the software that achieve a clean and well-formatted manuscript this signals to the publisher that they are working with a professional.

Word Processing Features Essential to Writers:

- Use **styles** to do the formatting work.
- Avoid using tabs and spaces to indent paragraphs. Use **style settings**.
- Save style settings as a **style set** to use for future projects.
- Format chapter headings so they show up correctly in the **navigator** panel and the outline view.
- Use '**find and replace**' to search for common formatting errors and to make sure the formatting is consistent throughout the document.

For each of the links or highlighted words in the lists in this introduction, you will find a corresponding chapter in the book. In these, I explain step by step how to achieve the formatting goal. Follow these steps and you will have a beautifully formatted manuscript that will make editors smile.

For the examples I use Microsoft Word 2010. Most of the information provided in this book also applied to Microsoft Word 2007 although some menus may be in slightly different places. If you use a previous version of Word, consider upgrading. The stand-alone Microsoft Word program is affordable. A serious writer needs up-to-date tools.

* You may also be interested in Formatting Manuscripts for Submission to Publishers and Agents: OpenOffice/LibreOffice. Available on Amazon.

Chapter One Preparing the Document

Formatting in Microsoft Word without a plan can sometimes be confusing. There are many features in the software that change the appearance of the document. This isn't always a good thing. If following the steps for formatting outlined in this book isn't producing the desired results, you might want to consider stripping all formatting from your document and starting fresh.

Remove formatting from the document:

Step 1

    1. Click the HOME panel. On the right end of the tool bar.
    2. Choose 'Select.'
    3. From the drop-down menu choose 'Select All,' or use the keyboard shortcut Ctrl+A.

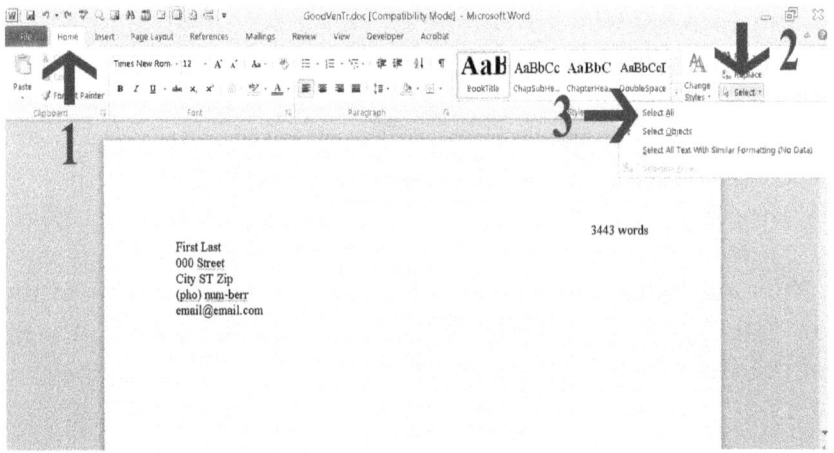

Step 2

The HOME panel is divided into several sections.

1. In the 'Styles' section there is a window that shows the various available styles.
2. Hover the mouse over the down arrow at the right edge of the window until you see the word 'more.' Click this.
3. Click 'Clear Formatting.' All formatting will be removed from the document.

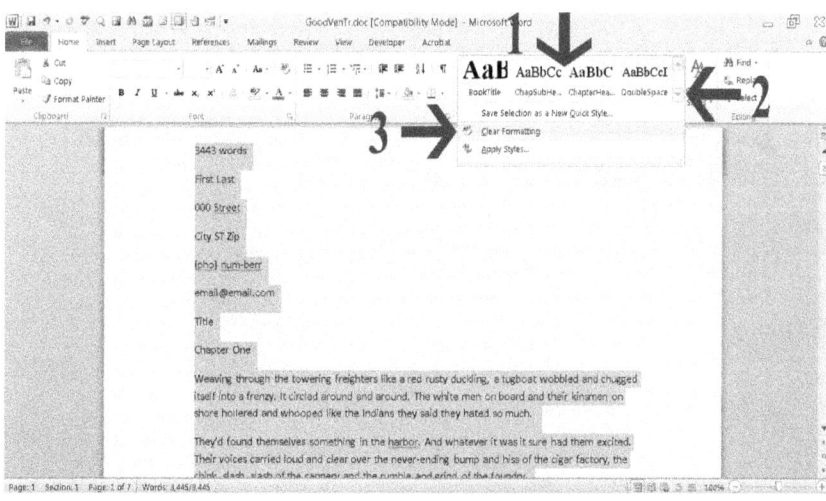

Chapter Two Page Size

The recommended page size for manuscript submission is a holdover from when most manuscripts were submitted on paper. 8 1/2 x 11 (letter size) is the most common size of printer (typing) paper. In the UK the standard size is A4 and is 8.3 x 11.7.

Some publishers print manuscripts. Even for those who read mainly on a computer screen, the standard paper size is a good way to keep documents consistent. It is also easy to read and fits a computer screen well.

Set the page size of the document:

Step 1

1. Click the PAGE LAYOUT panel.

2. Click 'Size.'

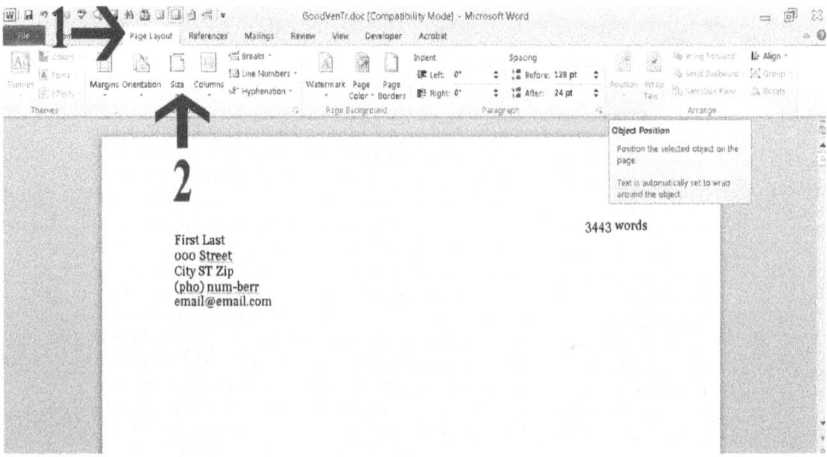

3. Choose the preset 8 1/2 x 11 or select 'More Paper Sizes' and select desired width and height

4. Select 'OK'

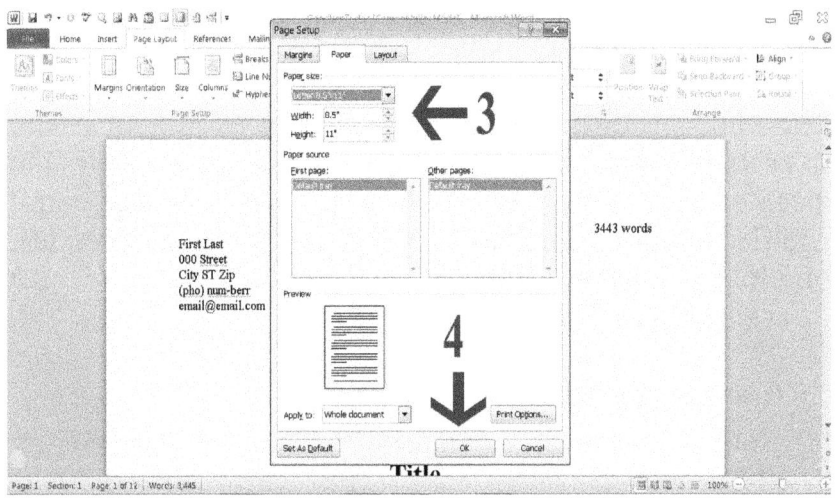

Chapter Three Margins

The appropriate sized margin makes a document easier to read. If the margins are too small, the reader swims in a sea of text. If they're too large, the inflated page count could seem daunting. Guidelines most frequently request one inch margins. Although, some publishers prefer 3/4 or even 1 1/4 margins.

Set the margins:

Step 1

1. Select the PAGE LAYOUT tab.

2. In the 'Page Setup' section click 'Margins.' Select 'Normal.' This has 1 inch margins all around.

3. For other choices, select 'Custom Margins.'

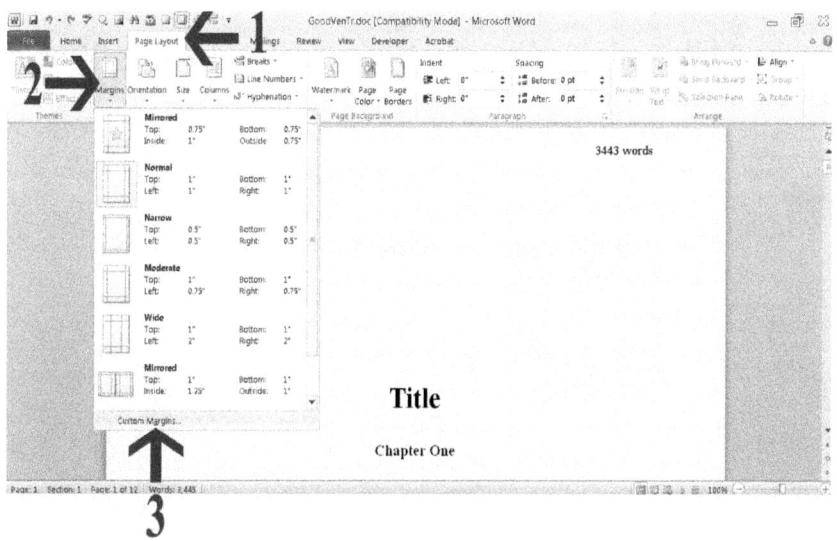

Step 2

1. Using the up-and-down arrows or

2. By typing in numbers choose the appropriate margin size. Don't include a gutter or any of the other options. These aren't relevant to formatting a manuscript for submission.

3. Make sure to apply the margins to the 'Whole Document.'

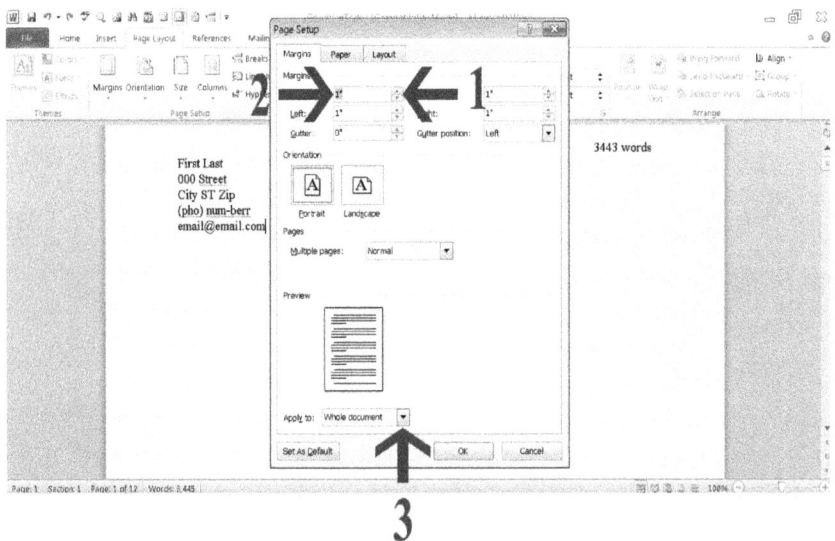

Chapter Four Font

Thousands of fonts are available for Microsoft Word. Most publishers prefer submissions in 12 pt. (point) Times New Roman or Courier New. To keep formatting consistent throughout the document, the font choice should be included include in the Style applied to sections of text. See Chapter Nine Styles (page 29).

In most cases, writers shouldn't format text without applying a style. Headings and subheadings should be larger than the body text. This is much easier to manage with Styles. Occasionally, situations arise where it's necessary to format font separately. I recommend reading this section but not applying it to your document. Manually formatting font doesn't produce the best results, but it is helpful to understand how it works.

Formatting font:

1. From the 'Editing' section on the HOME tab choose 'Select' then 'Select All' or Ctrl+A. (See diagram page 8).

2. From the 'Font' section on the HOME tab, select the desired font from the drop-down menu.

3. In the drop-down next to the font window, select the font size.

4. Avoid the temptation to use color. Set the font color to 'Automatic' or black.

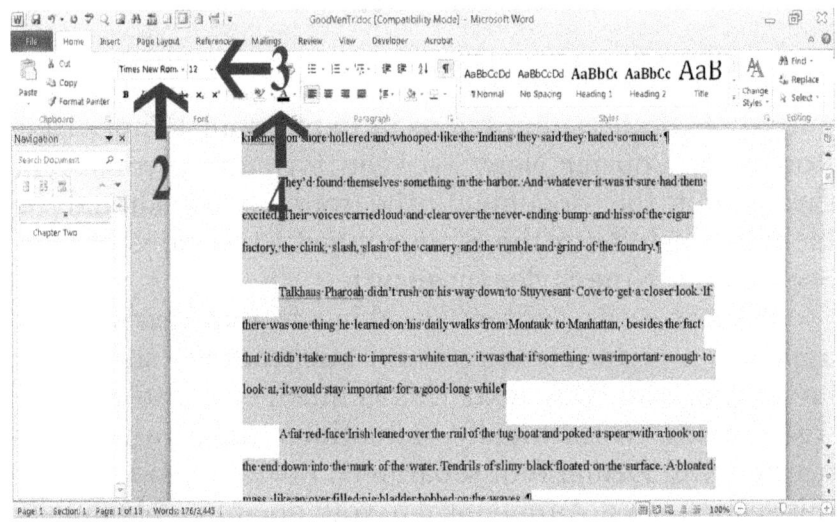

Chapter Five Line Spacing and Paragraph Indentation

Most publisher request that manuscripts be double-spaced. In the days of paper submissions, double-spacing gave editors room to make notes. Even though most editors do their work electronically now, the double-spaced formatting remains the norm. Perhaps because it is easy on the eyes. In most cases writers should not format line spacing without applying a style. Situations arise when it's necessary. Information about working with Styles is available in Chapter Nine Styles (page 29). I recommend reading this section but not applying it to your document. Manually formatting line spacing doesn't produce the best results, but it's a good idea to learn how line spacing works.

Formatting line spacing:

1. From the 'Editing' section on the HOME tab choose 'Select' then 'Select All' or Ctrl+A. (See diagram page 8)

2. From the 'Paragraph' section of the HOME tab click the 'Paragraph Settings' box.

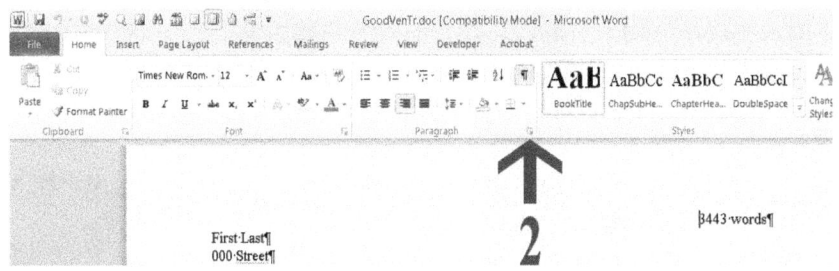

3. Choose 'Double' from the drop-down menu.

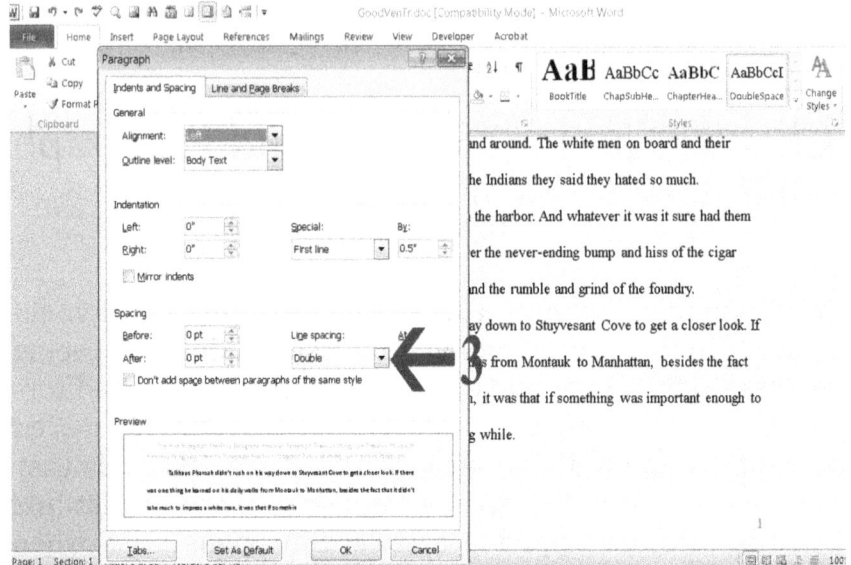

Publishers guidelines usually require that the first line of each paragraph be indented .5 of an inch. They also require that spaces between paragraphs, common in online writing, be removed. Paragraph formatting should be done with styles. For more information go to Chapter Nine Styles (page 29). I recommend against formatting an entire manuscript, especially a novel length work, manually. This explains the steps but is for illustration only.

Formatting paragraph indentation:

1. Select a paragraph by triple clicking or dragging the mouse over the text. Right click and choose 'paragraph' (if 'paragraph' isn't an option dismiss spelling or grammar corrections and try again) or from the HOME tab, click the arrow in the right lower corner of the 'paragraph' section.

2. In the paragraph pop-up, select 'First Line' and '0.5' from the drop-down menus.

3. Choose 'Double' line spacing.

4. Choose '0 pt' for both before and after.

5. Click OK.

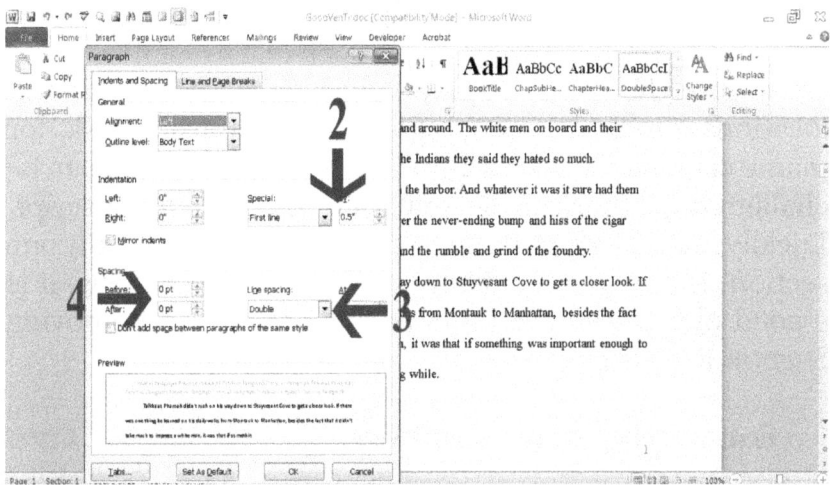

* Setting the spacing before and after paragraphs to '0' will ensure that there are no extra spaces between paragraphs. If you still have an extra space, see Chapter Eleven Find and Replace (page 39) for an easy way to remove paragraph breaks you've added by pressing ENTER.

Chapter Six Page Numbers

Even though Word displays page numbers in several locations on the screen, most publishers still ask for manuscript pages to be numbered. Page numbering can be challenging if there are several sections to the manuscript. Luckily, manuscripts at the submission stage have only one section. If the document contains 2 or more sections, it is a good idea to remove them at this point. (see Removing Section Breaks page 22).

Formatting page numbers:

1. Open either the header or footer by double clicking it. This can be done from any page in the document. (Also available from the INSERT tab) The view switches to the INSERT tab and opens the 'Header & Footer Tools.' Notice that this tool bar is only visible when a header or footer is open.

2. From the INSERT tab

3. Select 'Page Numbers' from the 'Header & Footer' section.

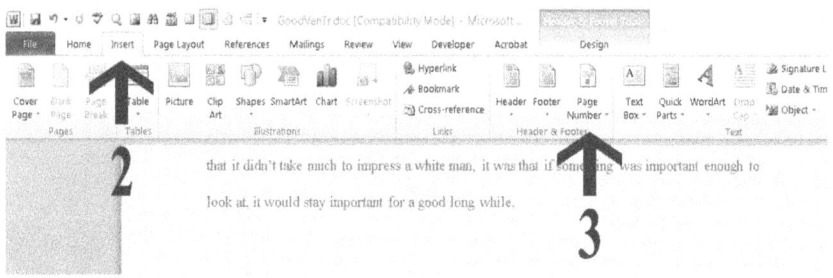

4. Select either 'Top of Page' or 'Bottom of Page' depending on the guidelines. (We'll choose 'Bottom of Page').

5. Select an appropriate formatting style. Centered or in the left corner are the standard places for page numbers.

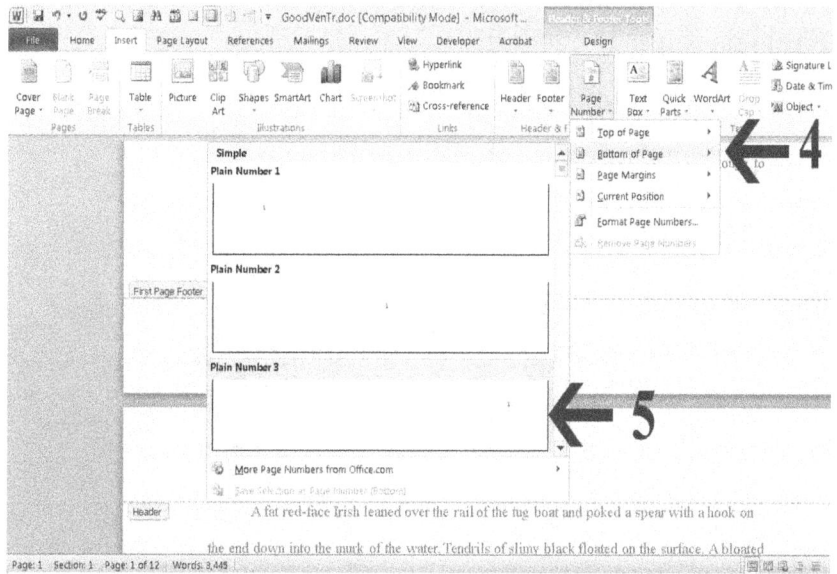

6. Once you have clicked on the style of page number to insert, the 'Header and Footer' menu changes. Page numbers should not appear on the first page of a manuscript. To removed them, check 'Different First Page' in the 'Options' section.

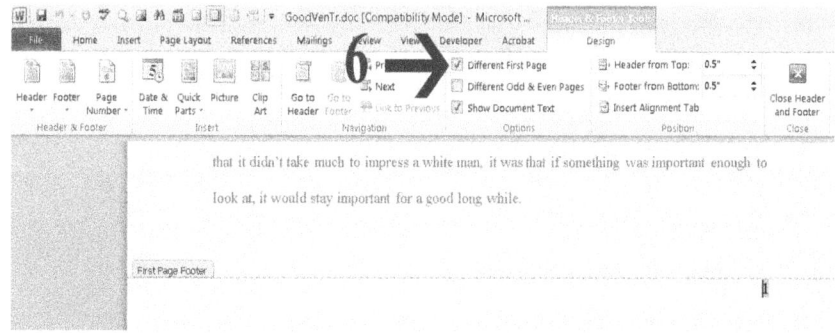

Formatting page number font

1. Select the number in the footer.

2. Click the HOME tab.

3. Change the font to match the rest of the document. (Times New Roman 12pt for example) See Chapter Four Font (page 14) if needed.

4. To close the header or footer click the 'Header and Footer Tools' tab then click 'close'

5. Or double click anywhere on the main text.

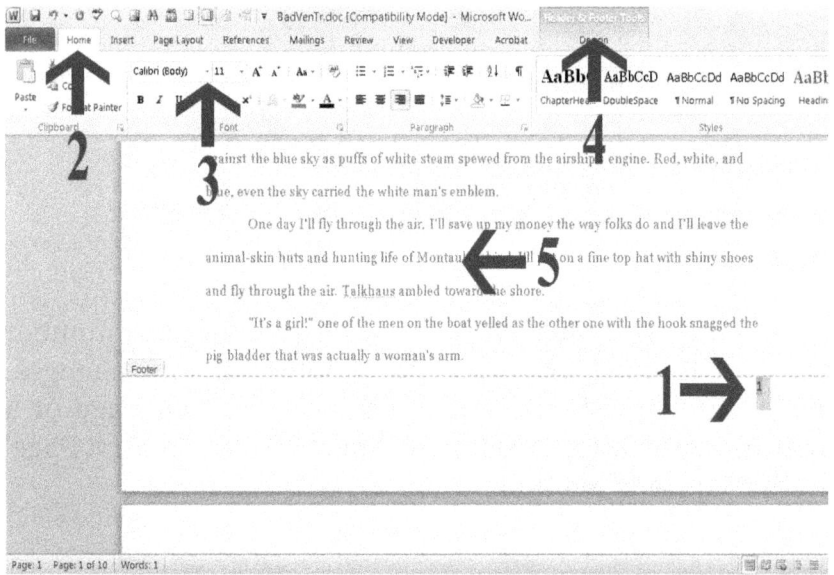

Removing section breaks

1. On the HOME tab

2. Click the pilcro (looks like a backward 'P') to 'Show/Hide.'

3. You can now see all of the hidden formatting symbols.

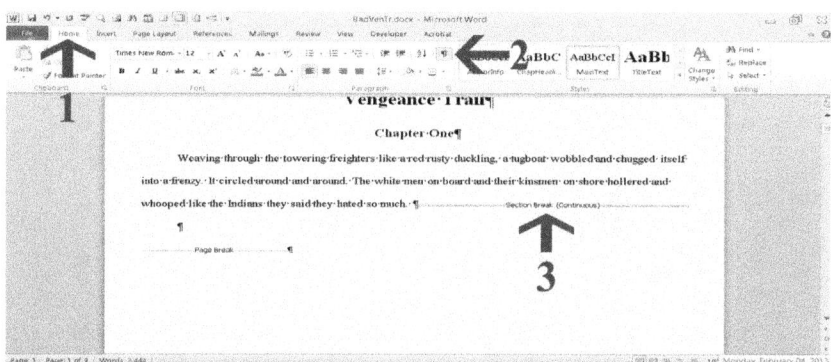

4. Click the VIEW tab.

5. In the 'Show' section, check the box for 'Navigation Pane.' The navigation pane appears on the left of the screen.

6. Click the arrow at the right of the search box and choose 'Advanced Find.'

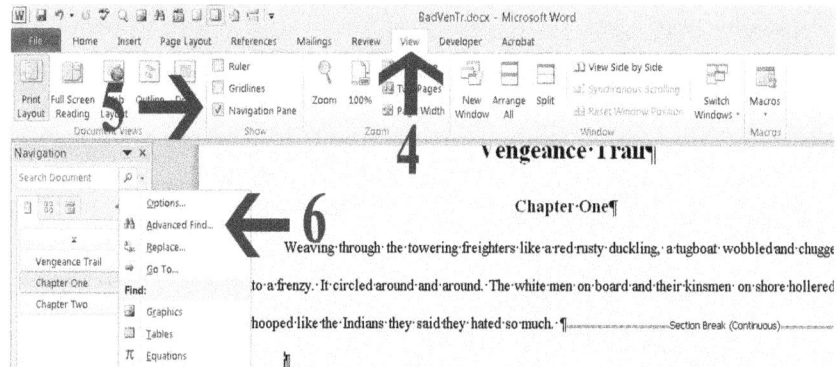

7. Click 'More>>' to reveal all of the 'Find and Replace' pop-up. (Text chages to '<<Less').

8. Click the 'Replace' tab.

9. At the bottom click 'Special.'

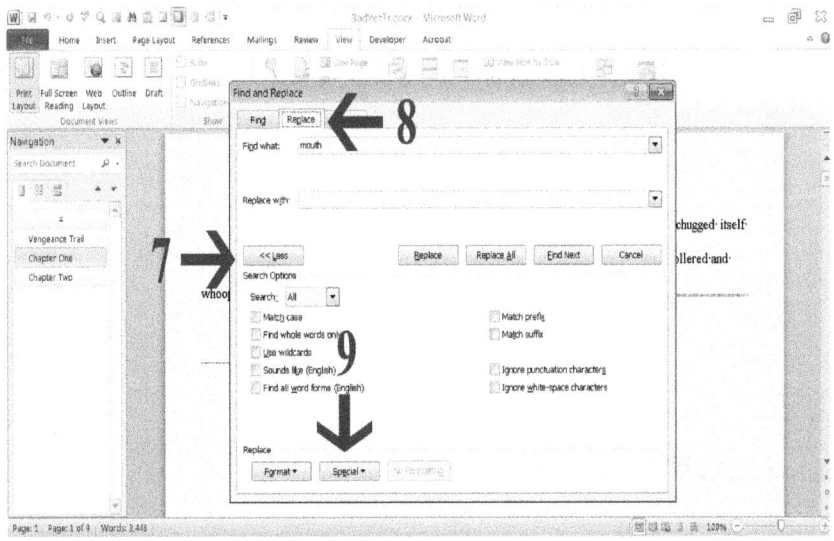

10. Select 'Section Break.'

11. In the 'Find what' field you should see the symbol for a section break. Leave the 'Replace with' field empty.

12. Click 'Find Next' to check each change or 'Replace all' to make all changes immediately.

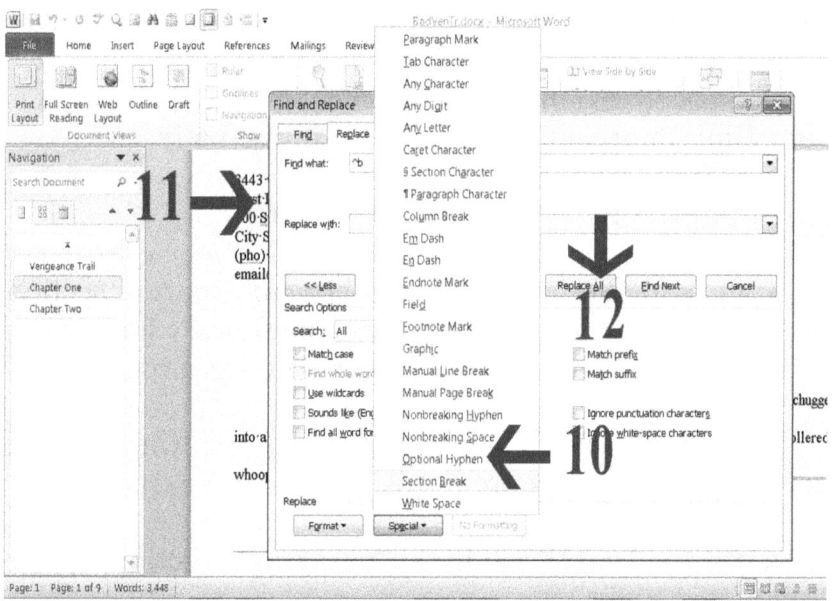

Chapter Seven Author Information

Author information goes on the first page of the manuscript in the top left corner. The word count goes in the top right corner. This information should be single-spaced. Because single-spaced text only appears once in the document, it is sometimes more efficient to format it manually.

Formatting author information:

1. Format the font in the author information section according to the publisher's guidelines. For more information about this see Chapter Four Font (page 14).

2. Select the word count only. For formatting to work correctly, the word count needs to be on a separate line.

3. On the HOME tab in the 'paragraph' section choose 'Align Text Right.'

4. Also in the 'Paragraph' section, choose 'Line Spacing.' Select 1.0 (single-spaced).

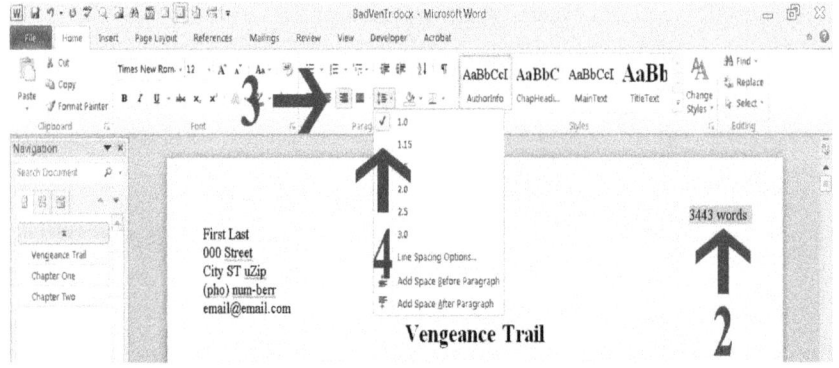

5. Repeat the steps in above for the rest of the author information. (Select all at once). Choose 'Align Text Left' for everything except the word count.

The copyright of your work belongs to you by default. During the submission process is not the appropriate time to worry much about it. Professional writers rarely include a copyright notice with a manuscript. Some editors may even see this as a mark of an amateur. If you can't sleep at night without putting a copyright notice on work you submit, place to notice in the author information section. Do not put the copyright notice on every page.

Chapter Eight Header

Publishers read several manuscripts at a time. Often, they will put one down and start another. The heading containing the writer's last name and the title of the novel or story helps the editor know, without searching for the information, which manuscript he or she is reading.

Formatting the heading:

1. Open the header by double clicking it. This can be done from any page in the document. (Also available from the INSERT tab). This opens the 'Header & Footer Tools.' Notice that this tool bar is only visible when a header or footer is open.

2. Type Last Name/Title in the header. If the title is long, choose one or two key words.

3. Format the font to match the rest of the document. Click on the HOME tab to find the formatting tools.

4. Align text right.

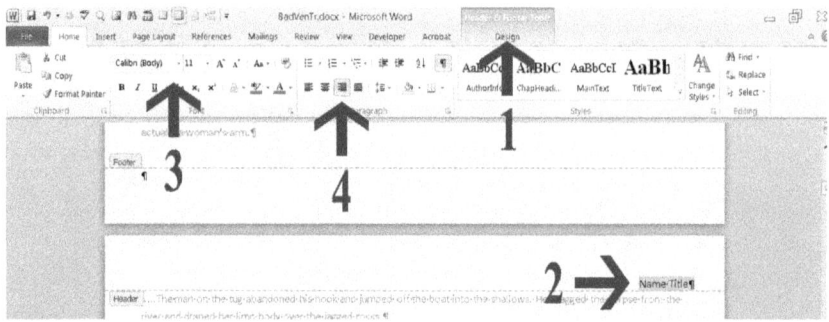

5. To return to the 'Header Footer Tools' after formatting the font, click the green tab.

6. The header should not appear on the first page of a manuscript. To remove it, check 'Different First Page' in the 'Options' section.

7. To close the header or footer click the button in the 'close' section of the 'Header and Footer Tools'

8. Or double click anywhere on the main text.

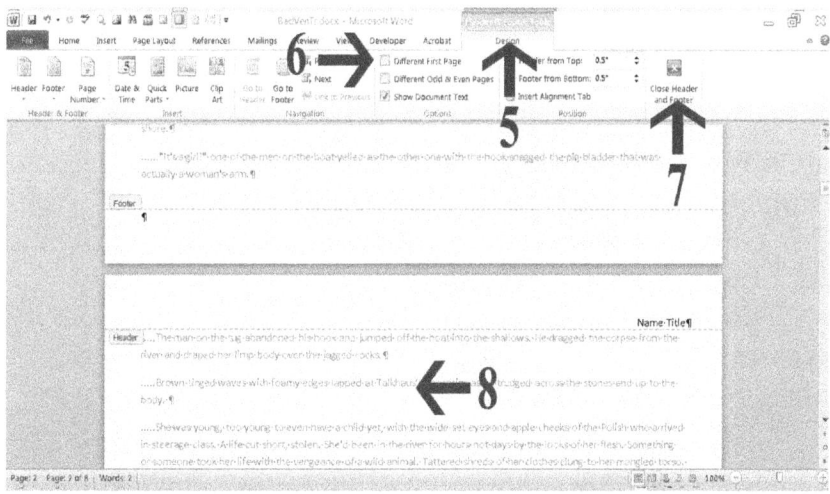

Chapter Nine Styles

Styles make document formatting easier. Groups of settings, font, spacing, paragraph indenting and much more can be applied to a chapter, paragraph or whole document.

Most manuscripts require four styles: author information (optional), title, chapter heading, and main text.

By default, Word uses 'Normal' style. Changing this style is possible, but on occasion, these changes lead to problems when saving the normal.dot template. To avoid this glitch, we will create a collection of styles specifically for formatting manuscripts.

The default style set has many unneeded styles. Before creating any new styles, delete unused ones. This step isn't absolutely necessary, but it does simplify the work space.

Deleting unused styles:

1. Clear all formatting from the document. To do this, see Chapter One Preparing the Document (page 8).

2. On the HOME tab

3. In the 'Styles' section

4. Remove the unused styles by right clicking each one.

5. Select 'Remove from Quick Style Gallery.'

6. Remove all styles. The 'Styles Window' will be empty.'

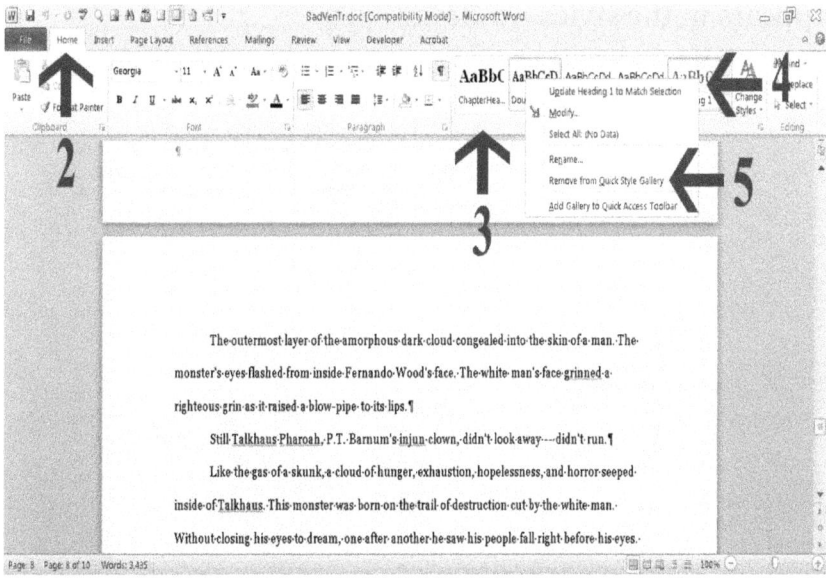

Creating the author information style:

1. Select one or two lines of the author information.

2. Format the font type and size, line spacing and indents according to the publisher's guidelines. See Chapter Four Font (page 14) and Chapter Five Line Spacing and Paragraph Indentation (page 16) if needed.

3. With the formatted text selected, click the down arrow on the right side of the styles window.

4. Choose 'Save Selection as a new Quick Style.' Name the new style something like AuthorInfo (names must be different from built in styles) and click OK. The style appears in the styles window.

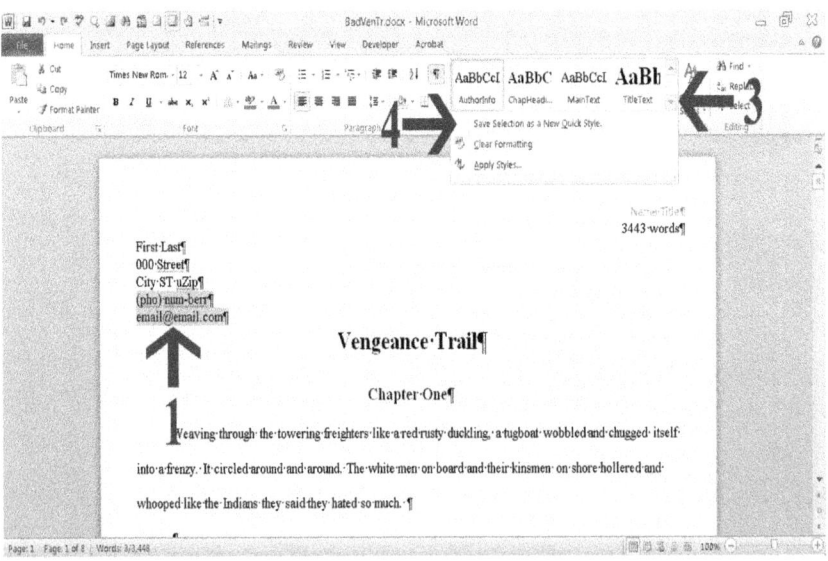

5. To apply the style to the rest of the author information, select the remaining author info text.

6. Click the AuthorInfo style in the styles window.

7. The word count belongs on the right side of the page. Although, it's possible to make a separate style it isn't necessary because there is only one instance of right alignment in the document. Select the word count and click 'Align Text Right' in the paragraph section of the HOME tab.

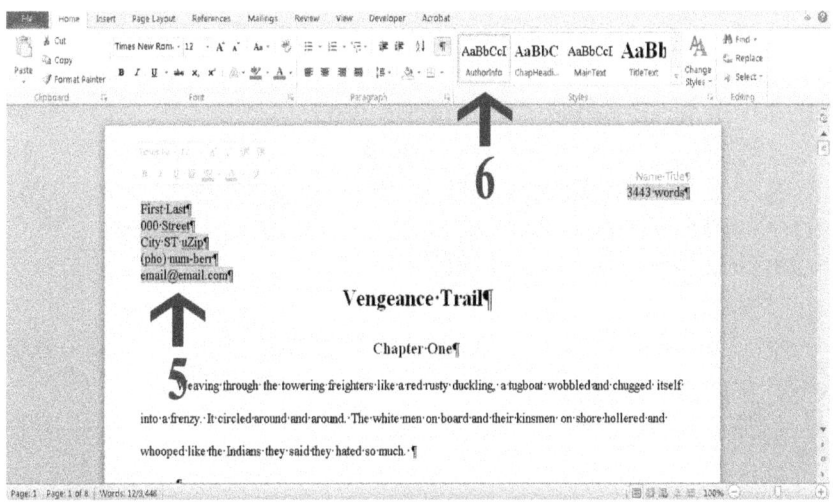

Like the word count, the title only appears once in the manuscript. In a correctly formatted document is should be 1/3 of the way down the page. It is possible to accomplish this by inserting several paragraph breaks. This will probably be acceptable to most publishers and may, in fact, be the preferred way to format the title. It's also possible to space the title correctly with styles.

Creating the title style:

1. Select the title.

2. Format the font type and font size. The title should be the largest text on the page. 20 pt. is a good size for a title although writer discretion is allowed.

3. With the formatted text selected, click the down arrow on the right side of the styles window. Choose 'Save Selection as a new Quick Style.'

4. Name the new style something like ManuscTitle (names must be different from built in styles) and click OK. The style appears in the styles window. See diagram (page 32).

5. To adjust the line spacing and place the title correctly, modify the style. To do this, right click the style in the style window and select 'Modify.' Click 'Format' then 'Paragraph.'

6. In the 'Spacing' section, type '84 pt.' before and 36 pt. after. This will add seven lines before and 3 after. (Each line is 12 pts.). Click OK.

7. Placing the title in the correct position on the page can also be achieved by manually entering paragraph breaks by pressing enter. While this is not recommended for chapter headings it is acceptable for a title because the title only appears once in the document.

Creating the chapter headings style:

1 Select the text for a chapter heading.

2. Format the font type and size. The chapter headings should have text larger than the body text but smaller than the title. 16 pt. is a good size for the chapter heading. Center or left align the text. Center alignment is the most common.

3. With the formatted text selected, click the down arrow on the right side of the styles window. Choose 'Save Selection as a new Quick Style.'

4. Name the new style something like ChapHeading (names must be different from built in styles) and click OK. The style appears in the styles window. See diagram (page 32).

5. Highlight each chapter heading and click the style in the style window to apply.

Adding chapter headings to navigator:

For ease of navigation in large documents, the chapter heading should appear in the navigator window. This is accomplished with formatting.

1. From the HOME panel

2. Right click ChapHeading in the style window and choose modify.

3. Click the 'Format' button at the bottom of the pop-up and select 'Paragraph.'

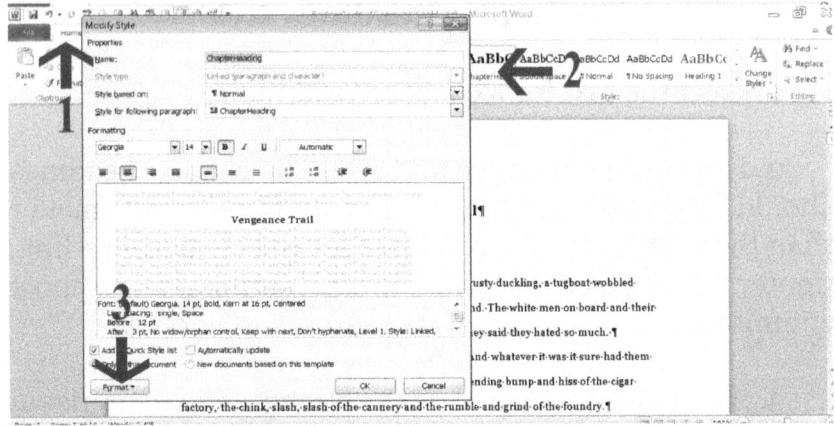

4. In the 'Outline level' drop-down menu

5. Choose 'Level 2.' ('Level 1' is the top level of an outline and may be reserved for the title, although, this isn't always the case).

6. Click OK. See Chapter Ten Navigator (page 38) for more information.

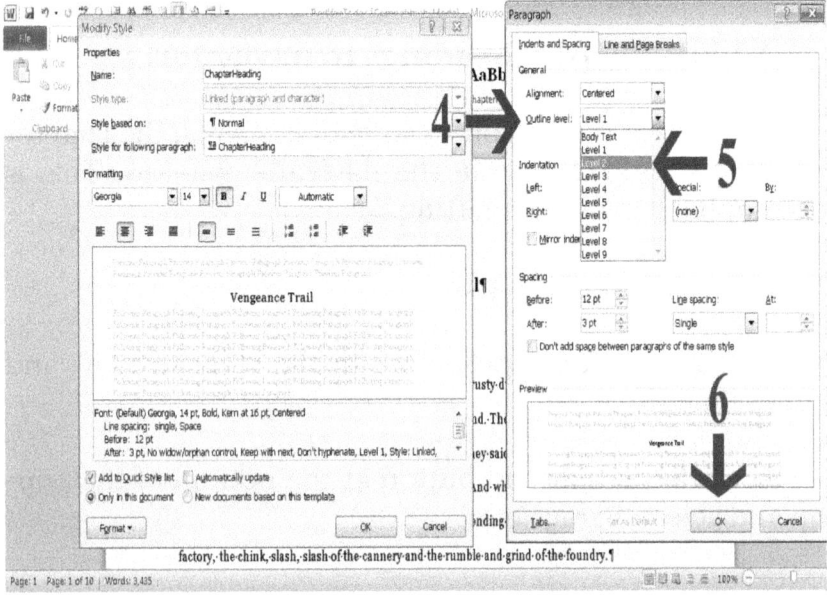

Creating the body text style:

1 Select the first sentence or paragraph in the body of the story.

2. Format the font type and font size according to the publisher's guidelines. 12 pt. Times New Roman is a good choice if the publisher hasn't specified.

3. With the formatted text selected, click the down arrow on the right side of the styles window. Choose 'Save Selection as a new Quick Style.'

4. Name the new style something like BodyText or MainText (names must be different from built in styles) and click OK. The style appears in the styles window. See diagram (page 32).

5. Before formatting the body of the manuscript, be aware that paragraphs formatted with more than fifty percent italic text will not retain the italicized words when the BodyText style is applied. If the document has large blocks of italicized text, temporarily formatting italicized words with a colored text or underlining may be advisable. This allows you to correct any auto-formatting errors without consulting the original document. If the document contains small amounts of italicized text, (less than fifty percent of the words in the sentence) there is no need to mark text formatted with italics unless the publisher's guidelines ask for italics to be underlined. See Chapter Eleven Search and Replace (page 39) for information about formatting italics efficently.

6. Select the body of the text making sure not to include chapter headings and click the style in the style window to apply.

Saving the style as a Style Set to use for future manuscripts:

Creating a style set specifically for manuscript submission will reduce the number of steps when formatting manuscripts in the future.

1. In the style window on the HOME tab, there should be four styles: AuthorInfo, ChapHeading, MainText and TitleText (the names of your styles may vary).

2. Click 'Change Styles' on the right side of the 'Styles' section.

3. Select 'Style Set.'

4. Select 'Save as a Quick Style Set.'

5. Name the style set something like 'ManuscriptFormat' and click 'Save.'

6. The next time you open Word, the option to load the style set you created will be available when you click 'Change Styles' then 'Style Sets' on the HOME tab.

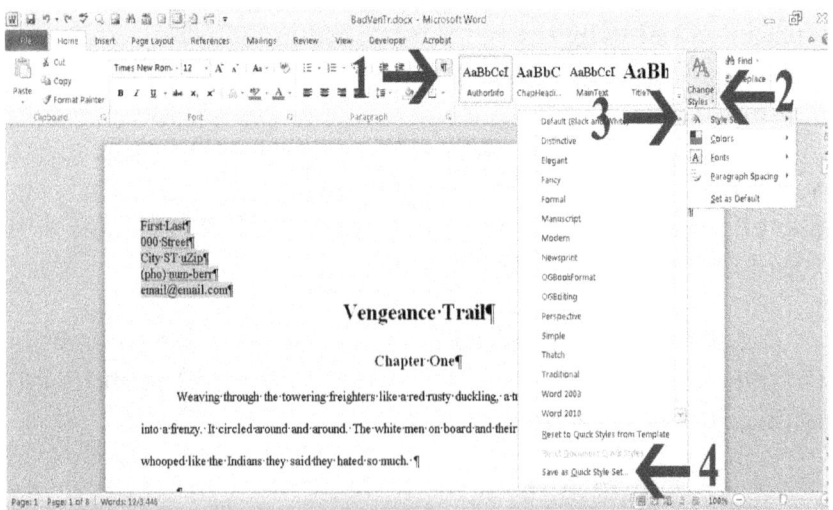

Chapter Ten Navigator

The navigator window is a helpful tool when navigating large documents. If the chapter heading is formatted so its outline level is 'Level 2' (See Chapter Nine Styles page 34) each chapter heading will appear in the navigation window. Clicking the chapter headings will jump to the corresponding section in the document.

All outline levels except 'body text' appear in the outline. 'Level 1' is the best choice for the title, 'Level 2' for chapter headings and 'Level 3' for chapter sub-headings. While formatting a manuscript for submission, more levels will probably not be needed.

Accessing the Navigation window:

1. Click the VIEW panel. Check the 'Navigation Pane' box in the 'Show' section. See diagram Chapter Six Page Numbers (page 22). The Navigation window appears in the left section of the screen.

2. Click the chapter headings to navigate the document.

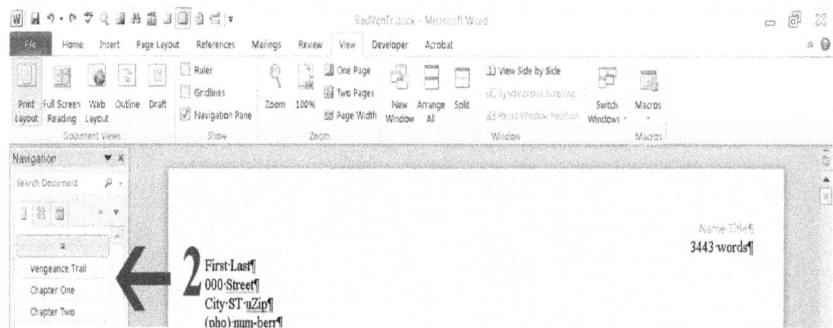

Chapter Eleven Find and Replace

Find and Replace is a tool that can help rid a document of many formatting errors. Sometimes fingers hit the keyboard wrong and sometimes writers have bad habits that they don't catch during proofreading. Once the document is formatted with a style sheet and all the publisher's specifications are met, writers can take one final step to improve their manuscript.

Viewing formatting errors:

1. Correcting formatting errors is easier when viewing hidden formatting marks. To view these, from the HOME tab click the pilcro. See diagram Chapter Six Page Numbers (page 22).

2. Click the VIEW tab and check the 'Navigation Pane' in the 'Show' section. See diagram Chapter Six Page Numbers (page 22).

Searching for formatting errors:

1. In the 'Search' bar click the drop-down arrow.

2. Select 'Advanced Find.'

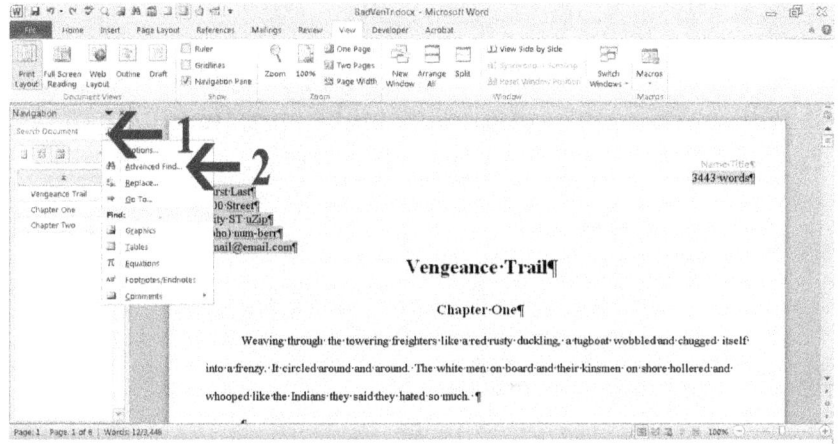

3. Click 'More>>.' Changes to '<<Less.'

4. Click 'Replace.'

5. Make sure that no queries are still active from previous searches. Check that there is no text under the 'Find what' or 'Replace with' fields.

6. If there is text, place the cursor in each of the fields and click 'No Formatting.' Also make sure that none of the boxes in 'Search Options' are checked.

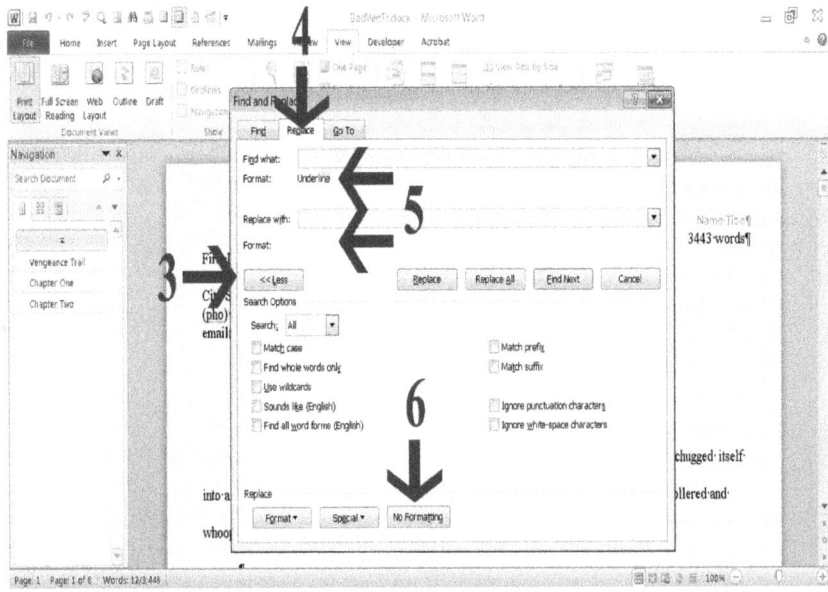

Removing formatting errors:

1. Remove all tabs. If you used tabs to indent paragraphs, the paragraph indentations will be too large once the style is applied. Place the cursor in the 'Find what' field and click 'Special.' Choose 'Tab Character.' Click 'Find Next' to check each change or 'Replace all' to make all changes immediately.

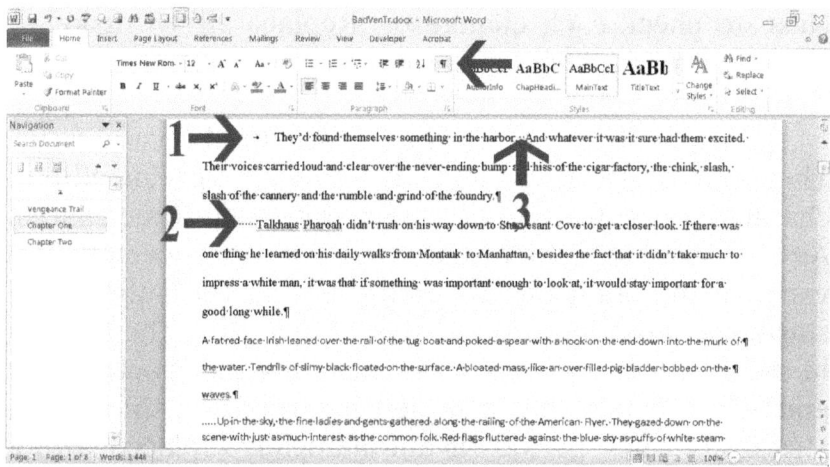

2. Remove multiple spaces. If you used five spaces to indent paragraphs, the paragraph indentations will also be too large. To remove extra spaces, place the cursor in the 'Find what' field press the space bar five times. In the 'Replace with' field place the cursor all the way to the left. Click 'Find Next' to check each change or 'Replace all' to make all changes immediately. In a long document it is easy to make a mistake when indenting with the space method. Sometimes you may have accidentally added six spaces or four spaces. Do a 'find and replace' for these too.

3. Many people learned to add two spaces after a period in typing class. This seems impossible to unlearn. To remove these double spaces, press the space bar twice with the cursor is in the 'Find what' field and once with

the cursor in the 'Replace with' field. Click 'Find Next' to check each change or 'Replace all' to make all changes immediately.

4. Remove extra spaces before paragraphs. From the 'Special' menu choose 'Paragraph Mark.' You will see a symbol in the 'Find what' field. Press the space bar once to add a space to the field. In the 'Replace with' field add only the paragraph symbol. Do not add a space. Click 'Find Next' to check each change or 'Replace all' to make all changes immediately.

5. Ellipses (three dots) can be formatted several ways. They can be three periods in a row, a special ellipsis character, or three periods alternating with three spaces. Any of these can have a space before or after, or not. This varies from publisher to publisher. At the submission stage, the most important thing is that all of the ellipses in the document are the same including the spacing after and before. When auto-complete is turned on in MS Word, a series of three periods is automatically replaced with a single character. If you use this feature, find an instance of this in your document (Or insert from the 'Symbols' section of the INSERT panel) and copy and paste it into the 'Replace with' field. In the 'Find what' field insert three periods. Click 'Find Next' to check each change or 'Replace all' to make all changes immediately.

6. Make double dashes, en dashes and em dashes consistent. Most publishers request double dashes instead of en or em dash characters in submissions. An en dash is as wide as the 'n' and em dash is as wide as an 'm.' These special characters are available from the INSERT pane in the 'Symbols' section. If you have smart formatting turned on, turn it off. Select an instance of an em or en dash and copy and paste into the 'Find what' field. Replace with a double dash.

7. Many publishers' guidelines ask for italicized words to be underlined. To search for italics place your cursor in the 'Find what' field and press CTRL + I. Put the cursor in the 'Replace with' field and click 'Format' and select 'Font.' In the pop-up choose the font, font style and the size. In the field for 'Underline style' choose 'Words only' or a solid line. Click 'Find Next' to check each change or 'Replace all' to make all changes immediately.

8. Search for double periods and replace with a single period.

9. Inspect all instances of double paragraph symbols to make sure all spacing is as intended.

10. Occasionally during copyediting or proofreading, a period is changed to a comma or vice versa. Sometimes one or the other doesn't get deleted. To catch this, search for period comma and comma period.

11. Scene Breaks should be centered and either three asterisks or three pound symbols with a space between each. Search for asterisks or pound signs without spaces. Also replace scene breaks that use more than three symbols.

* Extra Help: Each individual writer has a few mistakes they commonly make that slip through the spell check filter. Making a list of the errors and doing a 'Search and Replace' for each will ensure that editors only see your best writing.

Some common mistakes:

your/you're	whose/who's
its/it's	affect/effect
then/than	were/we're/where
lose/loose	their/they're/there
that/who	accept/except

About the Author

Kate Jonez is chief editor at Omnium Gatherum, a small press dedicated to providing unique dark fantasy fiction in print, ebook and audio formats, and the horror imprint Odium Media.

She also writes dark fantasy fiction. Her debut novel CANDY HOUSE will be available June 2013 from Evil Jester Press.

She provides book formatting, editing and cover design. Please contact her via her website http://bookdesign.katejonez.com.

www.ingramcontent.com/pod-product-compliance
Lightning Source LLC
Chambersburg PA
CBHW061303040426
42444CB00010B/2501